CHAGALL

Chagall

BY RAYMOND COGNIAT

CROWN PUBLISHERS, INC. · NEW YORK

Title-page: SELF–PORTRAIT OF THE ARTIST
(Detail) 1946 Oil

Translated from the French by
ANNE ROSS

PRINTED IN ITALY

VITEBSK. THE BLUE HOUSE, 1920 Oil 26″×38″ Musée des Beaux-Arts, Liège

INTRODUCTION

Numerous and important works have already been written about Chagall, and this book is not concerned with repeating what others have said — often very well — about him, nor with a chronological catalogue of the events of his life, but will be confined to such allusions as are necessary to illustrate his theories. The intention is to consider Chagall's art by studying the different facets of the man and his work, not in the logical sequence of events but in their spiritual and aesthetic components. It is hard to avoid excessive factual precision, and to Chagall himself dates, actions and definitions are unimportant. In explaining or justifying him one is often tempted to postulate opposite ideas — to describe him as bold and timid, frank and cunning, enthusiastic and sceptical. This uncertainty about him is borne out by the facts themselves.

Uncertainty begins with his birth-date, officially given as 1887 but questioned by the painter himself, who spoke of an alteration in his official papers made at the instigation of his parents. In his paintings, the facts are even vaguer, as he altered or completed some pictures years after their first appear-

Self-portrait, Grimacing, 1920
Pencil sketch
Private collection

ance, others he dated approximately, trusting to his memory alone, and others again show his whimsical habit of flouting conventions. As an example, for Chagall the year begins, not on 1st January, but after the summer holidays, and finishes with the following year's holidays — presumably a relic from his childhood — and he has often dated pictures according to this personal calendar. This is no mere caprice or desire to be different: it exactly illustrates one of Chagall's most fundamental and attractive characteristics — his ability to shape reality to his own feelings, not from an instinct to rebel or provoke, but just to make it conform to his inner spiritual logic. One should not therefore be surprised if, when asked to explain some obscure point in one of his paintings, he should seem puzzled and unwilling to reply, because to him there is nothing unrealistic in the world he creates.

These observations help one to approach Chagall's art in the correct light, which is to ignore the æsthetic systems within which most art-historians have tried to confine him. I have tried instead to explain his autonomy within contemporary art and his inner logic, which is highly superior to these systems. However independent he may be, Chagall's art does of course originate in certain disciplines and influences and certain spiritual and technical environments which he has absorbed during the course of his life. In his personality are combined both the individualism and the influences, because he would never have enjoyed such widespread success if the public had not discerned something con-

6

At the Window, 1908 Pencil and water-colour 10" × 7 1/2 Private collection

THE PAINTER'S FATHER
circa 1907
Chinese ink and sepia
drawing 9″ × 7″
Private collection
Moscow
◁

THE MOTHER, 1914 ▷
Oil 13 $\frac{1}{2}$″ × 11 $\frac{1}{2}$
Artist's collection

THE JEW, IN PINK, 1914-15   Oil 39¹⁄₂″ × 32″   Hermitage Museum, Leningrad

THE JEW, IN GREEN, 1914
Oil 39½″ × 32″ Charles im Obersteg Collection, Geneva

ABOVE THE TOWN, 1917
Oil 59 1/8″ × 82 3/4″ Tretiakov State Gallery, Moscow

12

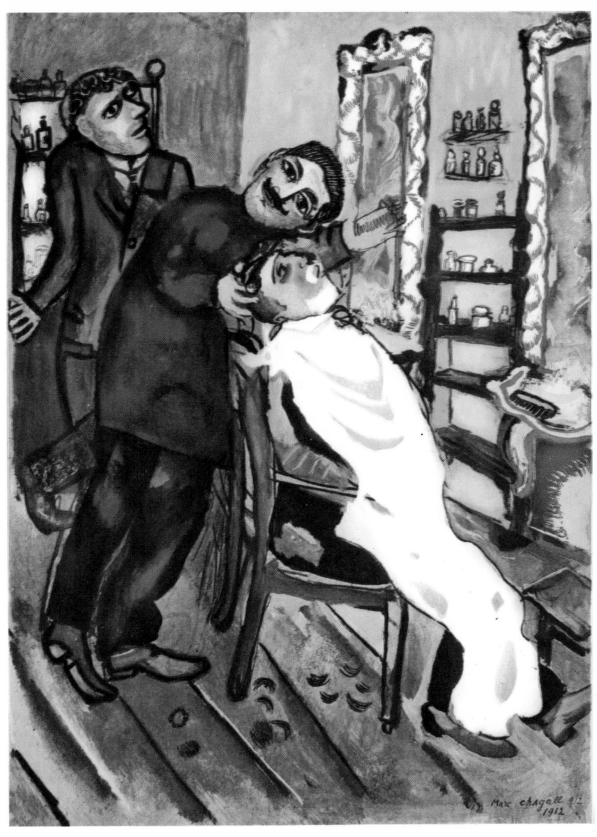

AT THE BARBER'S, 1912   Gouache 13¼ × 9½″   Private collection

THE SPOONFUL OF MILK, 1912   Gouache 15″ × 12¼″   Collection of Dr. Paul Hänggi, Basle

The Walk, 1922   Dry-point 10″ × 7¹/₂″

THE GIANT WHEEL, 1911–12
Oil 35 1/2″ × 23 1/2″   Private collection, London

THE RESTING POET, 1915 Oil 30¼″ × 28¼″
Tate Gallery, London. Formerly in the collection of R. de la Fresnaye

THE NUDE, ABOVE VITEBSK, 1933
Oil 34 1/4″ × 44 1/2″ Private collection, Paris

THE BRIDAL PAIR AT THE EIFFEL TOWER, 1938
Oil 58 1/4″ × 57″   Artist's collection

Sketch of a costume for "The Miniatures" by Sholem Aleichem about 1919
Pencil, ink and water-colour 11″ × 7¹⁄₆″

REBECCA GIVING ABRAHAM'S SERVANT A DRINK, 1931
Oil and gouache 26½″ × 20″ Artist's collection

22

JOSEPH THE SHEPHERD, 1931
Oil and gouache 25$\frac{1}{2}$″ × 20″   Artist's collection   23

temporary in his works. He has been regarded variously as a mere painter of pictures, an oriental story-teller, or again as a sort of precursor of surrealism, because his personal conception of reality has led him to portray unrealistic figures in unexpected surroundings. But above all this raconteur tells tales which are strictly his own, and the spectator can feel free to invent whatever the image in them suggests to him. This pre-surrealist surrealism never leads to morbid recollections or a wealth of uneasy emotions. His melancholy and disquiet are never degrading to mankind and never spring from shameful secrets; therefore they have little in common with either the oriental artist or the tendencies of the inter-war period, with its invasion of the subconscious. In fact Chagall is more individual in thought and graphic style than any other great modern artist, either because of his seeming naïvety or because of the ease with which this can pass for awkwardness. In many of his earlier pictures and in many of his drawings and engravings he shows such precision in suggesting a figure or a perspective that his desire to escape from academic rigours was clearly intentional.

When studying Chagall one must first establish the spiritual climate, the poetic world, which obviously sprang from his experiences and his heredity, but above all from his own temperament and from the extent to which he absorbed external impressions and influences. At the beginning of his book on Chagall, Franz Meyer has pointed out how in its unconventional aspect his work is related to the hassidic movement which inspired the world of his childhood and youth, and in fact had impressed itself on Eastern European Jews since the eighteenth century. For Chagall this is one of the deepest sources, not of inspiration, but of a certain spiritual attitude. Meyer explains this relationship with hassidism very well: " So far from returning to this influence of his youth as the painter of hassidism, he has freed himself from it in order simply to paint, independently of movements or doctrines; nevertheless the hassidic spirit is still the basis and source of nourishment of his art ".

All Chagall's works must be considered in the light both of his personal inspiration, and of contemporary material and intellectual conditions. Very early in his career — before the 1914-18 war — he lived among artists who were destroying recognized artistic ideas in order to create a new plastic universe. He was well placed to play his part in this transformation.

The fauvist and cubist styles which characterize Chagall's paintings during his first stay in Paris (where he arrived in 1910) are very different from French fauvism and cubism, if only because of the symbolic element which is found in all his works and which links all his periods. However strongly he felt himself a part of Parisian life, he never lost his original characteristics, and the term " École de Paris " was coined for him more than for anyone else, to indicate the artist's intimacy with French society combined with a spiritual and stylistic independence. The aesthetic influences mentioned in connection with certain periods in Chagall's art, such as fauvism, cubism and surrealism, never restricted him, but rather acted as channels through which he could assert and free himself and above all achieve full self-expression — that expansive, colourful, tender and happy artistry in which he conceived his later works. Though these have a quality which reminds one of illuminations, they in fact include some works of gigantic proportions, such as murals or stained-glass windows. At every stage his artistry seems complete and accomplished, yet vulnerable to change. Looking bach with detachment one can see that only in recent years has Chagall transcended his troubles, and that his serenity does not only belong to a moment in time. He himself seems conscious of this state of fulfilment — his smile is broader now than it has ever been and his works, now denser, richer and more simplified, no longer appear to be in a state of evolution. He seems to understand the meaning of his life. In this context it is appropriate to quote part of a talk he gave in May, 1963, when touring

LONELINESS, 1933   Oil 40¼" × 55"   Tel-Aviv Museum, Israel

THE POURIM   Oil $19^1/_2'' \times 27^1/_2''$
Brooklyn Museum of Art.   Legacy of Louis E. Stern

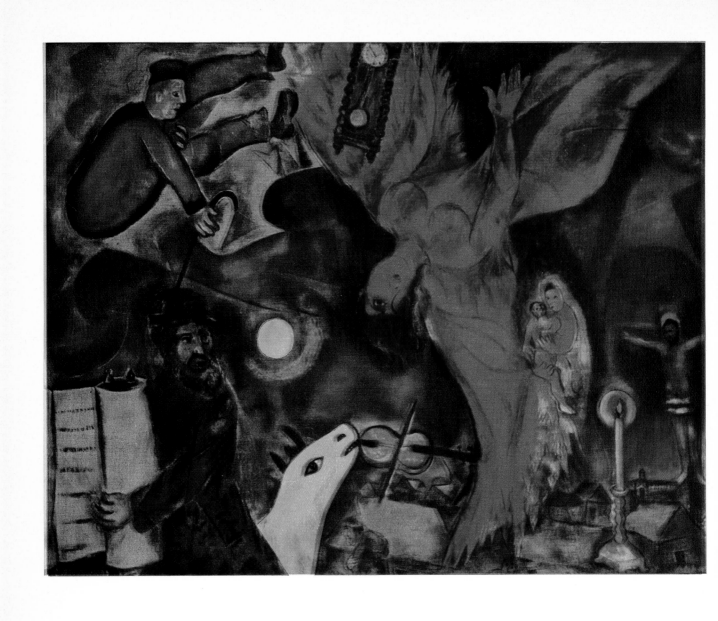

DESCENT OF THE ANGEL, 1923-33-47
Oil 58″ × 74¹/₂″ Museum of Art, (Loan) Basle

America; a talk which is no mere formal speech of thanks but resembles an assessment of his past and present works.

" *The birth of impressionism threw open a window for us and cast the light of a rainbow across the horizon of our world. Although this world had been differently and more intensely coloured, it seems in general to have become narrower than, for instance, Courbet's naturalistic world, in the same way that Courbet's naturalism became narrower than Delacroix's romanticism. Delacroix's world, in its turn, was more declamatory and narrower than the neo-classical world of David and Ingres. I will stop there. After impressionism came the cubist world, which led us into the geometric inwardness of things, just as later abstract art led us into the smaller elements of matter. So the harmonies and dimensions of life seem to be gradually contracting. To continue like this would seem to mean moving forward towards a progressive narrowing of life. What has happened?*

" *Let us consider what is genuine in the trappings of our life. The world is ours from the moment of our birth and we seem to be equipped from our very beginning. For about two thousand years a reserve of energy has fed and supported us, and filled our lives, but during the last century a split has opened in this reserve, and its components have begun to disintegrate: God, perspective, colour, the Bible, shape, line, traditions, the so-called humanities, love, devotion, family, school, education, the prophets and Christ himself. Have I too, perhaps, doubted in my time? I painted pictures upside down, decapitated people and dissected them, scattering the pieces in the air, all in the name of another perspective, another kind of picture composition and another formalism.*

" *Our world, little by little, has come to look like a microcosm on which we microscopic creatures swarm as we cling to small particles of our nature, until the tinier particles engulf us and finally the atom itself.*

" *Does not this pseudo-scientific ascendancy over nature restrict the fund of poetry by draining the soul, and deprive mankind of even the physical gifts of calm and repose? Does not man thus eliminate from his organism the moral purpose of his life and creation? During the last few years I have often discussed so-called chemistry, genuine colour and texture as though they were yardsticks of authenticity. An exceptionally sharp eye might see that a genuine colour or texture automatically comprises every possible technique as well as a moral and philosophical content. Any moral crisis is a crisis of colour, texture, blood and the elements, of speech, vibration, etc. — the materials with which art, like life, is constructed. Even when mountains of colour are piled on a canvas, if one can discern no single object even through great sound and vibration, this will not necessarily give authenticity.*

" *In my opinion Cimabue's colour-texture alone started a revolution in Byzantine art, just as another colour of Giotto's, equally authentic (I stress this word in its chemical sense) started another moral and artistic revolution. In the same way later on Masaccio and others... I repeat, it is not a view of the world — that is, a literary or symbolic factor — which effects such a change, but blood itself, a certain chemistry in nature, in things and even in human awareness. This conception of authenticity can be seen in all spheres.*"

HIS COUNTRIES

RUSSIA. — However independent Chagall may seem to be from the aesthetic currents among which he has lived, his art has necessarily been shaped by external influences. His autonomy springs from a deeply original personality, which is yet extremely sensitive and therefore cannot be indifferent to its surroundings. At the same time his art is so unified that one is tempted not to connect it to ancillary events or spectacular episodes, but instead just to explain it as one does that of a great artist of the past, whose life is only known in outline. One tries to treat Chagall less as a contemporary than as a legendary character, and to maintain this theory when linking him with the larger, general scheme of things. From this point of view one must particularly consider the countries and environments in which he has lived.

His childhood in the small Russian town of Vitebsk has been described so often that one need not stress the details; it is enough to review the special circumstances of the Jewish communities in Russia at the turn of the last century. The Biblical world of Chagall's childhood, which he has remembered with affection and vague disquiet ever since, is a world which in spite of its secular past is coming to an end, and in which it was impossible to visualize what modern life would be like. It wove about the child Marc Chagall an emotional atmosphere from which he will never escape, but simultaneously aroused in him a desire not to remain imprisoned in the hard, monotonous life of his father, but to escape into a world commensurate with his dreams. When his school-friends, seeing his drawings, called him an artist, nothing could have satisfied him more; however the intention of becoming an "artist" was in itself unusual, for the iconoclastic principles of his environment were an obstacle which he decided to surmount. His first lessons were too academic to correspond to his instinctive conception of art, or to help his artistic temperament to grow and expand.

Chagall's early years did not prepare him for either the social or æsthetic problems of modern life, which faced him before he had needed any outside help. Even when he left home for St. Petersburg in 1907 to start his formal career as a painter, he escaped the environment and influences of his family without immediately making contact with people or events which could help him to envisage a way to realize his dreams of a new world. It was probably when working as a part-time art teacher in order to earn a modest living that he first felt he was being true to himself, rather than when he was learning from too traditional masters.

However when he became a pupil of Roerich — known in the west almost exclusively for the sets he designed several years later for Diaghilev's Ballets Russes — Chagall began his professional career with the support of art-loving friends. He was already aware of the limits to the amount he could be taught by others, and knew that his independent work was much better than what he did in the class. This situation was accentuated when he became a pupil of Léon Bakst, with whom he remained until 1910.

From that moment on Chagall entered into the mainstream of contemporary art, without shaking off his past but turning it from a burden into a firm basis and support. His apprenticeship over, Russia had played a memorable initial role in his life.

★   ★   ★

Returning home several years later, in 1914, he spent a lengthy period in Russia, retained there by the outbreak of war. The 1917 Revolution needed new men and fresh ideas, and Chagall had already earned an avant-garde reputation in Europe. Thanks to Lounatcharsky, who had known him in Paris and was now People's Commissar for Education and Culture, Chagall became Fine Arts Commissar for Vitebsk. This was a new departure for him and a new experience. His actions were no longer self-centred, but acquired new and wider dimensions. Adventure was a daily occurrence and the previously impracticable became the accepted course. Having left his country diffident and unknown, he returned famous and authoritative. He lived personally and passionately through the Revolution which had its echo in himself; he hoped for a new, and probably better world, because his humble origins and membership of an unofficial religion were no longer hindrances.

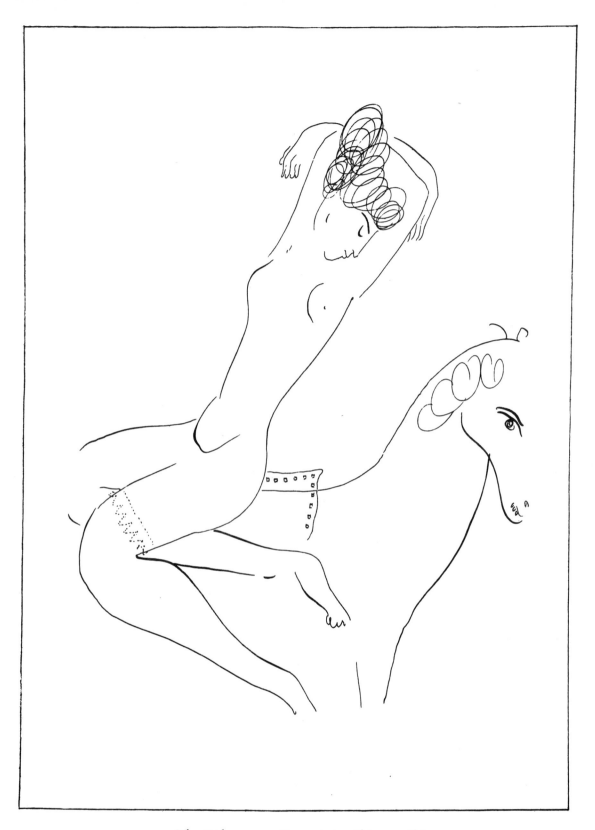

The Rider, 1929   Dry-point 14 $\frac{3}{4}$″ $\times$ 11 $\frac{3}{4}$″

1918

Marc
chagal

THE AGED LION. FROM THE FABLES OF LA FONTAINE, 1926-27
Gouache   Collection of Mme. Max Harari, Paris

WOMAN WITH PIGS Gouache 24 ¹/₂″ × 18 ³/₄″ Collection of E. J. van Visselingh & Co., Amsterdam

THE JUGGLER, 1943   Oil 43 1/2″ × 31″
Collection of Mrs. G. Chapman-Goodspread, New York

SPRING. (Goat with Violin) Gouache and pastel 30″ × 23″
Museum of Modern Art, Sao Paulo, Brazil. Donated by Nelson Rockefeller

Nude at the Window, 1953-54 Lithograph 16¹/₂″ × 22¹/₂″ Published by Aimé Maeght, Paris

He accepted freedom like an expansion of himself, for at this moment everything conspired to give him a feeling of fulfilment: he married Bella, organized a great popular fête, paved the streets of his home town and in 1918 obtained authorization and money to open a College of Arts in Vitebsk. Here he could spread his ideas and invite his friends — Doboushinsky, Lissitzky, Pougny and later Malevitch — to join him in teaching.

The very success of this enterprise contained the seeds of its failure. Malevitch's arrival had tragic consequences for Chagall's ideals, because these two artists' ideas were naturally as diametrically opposed as their works. Even in their bold originality they differed fundamentally, and Chagall tried briefly to incorporate Malevitch's geometric forms, such as triangles and rectangles, into his canvases. He of course eliminated their rigidity and density, and made them fly like lovers, ethereal in their joy. The conflict became so intense and insoluble that Chagall resigned, and in spite of pressure from his supporters left Vitebsk for Moscow in 1920.

This pleasant epoch was, however, not in vain, for it left its mark on Chagall's works. He had acquired a new feeling for space and a new unrealistic reality. His poetic output had until this point been introspective, but now became more lively and redolent of his pleasure in liberty and life. This is the period of the flying lovers and the realization of dreams. Of his previous realism there remained only the sense of the humanity in everything, a humanity which was no longer confined to modest, rustic surroundings and a tender, rather heavy atmosphere, but blossomed out in free, fresh air and in a continuous flow of lighter colours. All his thought now turned to absorbing and even creating a spiritual and plastic universe of his own.

After this happy period, followed by compensations such as the esteem in which he was still held, there came a time of sadness and loneliness. He found himself uncomfortably poised between the new geometric abstractions of the avant-garde and the reaction in favour of the academic painters. He consoled himself with his successes in the theatre and his teaching work in a colony of war-orphans, though he engaged in these occupations for want of anything better.

The wheel had come full-circle, and the difficulties and lack of understanding he had met in his early years were joined by those of his second and last period in Russia. Yet between the two, Chagall had already finished the first part of his artistic apprenticeship, and during the second Russian period he took his first steps on the ladder of fame. Russia is the country of his origins: he was still in Russia when he began his career and abandoned his childhood heritage, and he returned to savour the illusion of power and effective action — or perhaps to meet with their negation.

Nude with a Basket of Fruit, 1953-54 Lithograph 25 ⅝″ × 16 ½″ Published by Aimé Maeght, Paris

"BONJOUR PARIS"   Pastel 24 $\frac{1}{2}$" × 18 $\frac{1}{8}$"   Private collection, Paris

The Eiffel Tower and the Two Horses   Dry-point 11″ × 8¹/₈″   Published by VVV, New York, 1943

FRANCE. — We have studied Chagall in Russia under the stress of various social circumstances, whether the mystical disciplines of the Biblical world of his childhood and adolescence, or the revolutionary disciplines of the Soviet regime. Russia is physically and spiritually his native country, the land of his artistic education and of his submission to external pressures; the land where he learnt to what extent he could tolerate such pressures.

His second motherland, essential to one's understanding of Chagall, was France, the land of his freedom — freedom to invest reality with every kind of unreality — and of his expansion — the widespread search for himself as an artist through the various stages of his life. When he first arrived in Paris from St. Petersburg in 1910, Chagall knew what he was looking for; in Russia he had heard the echoes of the violent upheavals in the heart of artistic life in the west, and he deliberately chose Paris as his focal and starting point.

The sudden gust of freedom which blew through him from his first moment in Paris took on various forms. Fauvism and cubism were in full spate and the exotic atmosphere of Eastern Europe had become fashionable, due both to the Balkan War and to Diaghilev's Ballets Russes. Everything conspired to place Chagall in circumstances favourable to what he had both to offer and to receive. In fact he brought no empty mind to Paris, but a richness all his own, still latent but ready to be revealed. He sought in Paris fertilization rather than instruction, as is clear from his success in preserving a considerable degree of independent authority among the various changing artistic modes.

The first movement to touch him directly was fauvism, with its colour techniques, but his fauvism is strictly personal, and no mere reflection of Matisse, Derain or Braque. He continued to paint pictures evocative of Russian history, or juxtapositions of more or less imaginary figures. The importance he gives to the human element and the mobile facial expressions he creates show an affinity with German impressionism without its cynical cruelty. The lyrical ardour of his brush-work in some paintings of this period seems to hint at Soutine, but a happy Soutine, not obsessed with dramatizing his solitude. Chagall turned the joy he found in Paris into livelier, more varied, more harmonious and more vibrant colours than he had used previously, without however denying his Russian origins, for his favourite subjects were always evocations of his native land, and they give him a special position among his French contemporaries as an artist of great humanity.

When he was tempted away from fauvism by the novelty of cubism, he still infused this new style with his illusory haze of colours. He tried to invest his all-embracing, tender gestures with more abrupt geometric rhythms, but far from accepting the domination of the latter, he wove them into a dream-like gossamer. Cubism was in fact no rigid discipline to Chagall, but rather a popular medium for his imagination — an original way to summarize and assemble his imaginary world. Perhaps he really thought he was introducing a newly-discovered order into his art. Because he had become very friendly with Robert Delaunay, and like him painted the Eiffel Tower and the Giant Wheel, no doubt he thought he was basing his work on mathematical construction, but in fact Delaunay was also more an impulsive than a theoretical artist, more a poet of colour than an aesthetician. It is easy to imagine their impassioned discussions as each found in the other a partner ill-suited to conform to other people's ideas. However lyrical and explosive he had become, Chagall's art from that moment on was an end in itself, dependent on nothing and nobody, not even the much admired Cézanne. He enlisted no followers, to imitate him clumsily without the personal spark which can give charm to the slightest piece of work. The trend in contemporary ideas was towards concentra-

The Night of Scheherazade   Black plate from the original lithograph in the "Arabian Nights" published by Pantheon Books, New York, 1948

tion, whereas Chagall's need is for expansion — one facet perhaps of his Slav generosity. His life and works so exactly mirror the man himself that one could write a symbolic story or a realistic novel on the subject: he lived the true legendary pre-1914 Bohemian life, lodging in "La Ruche", that extraordinary, ramshackle building hidden away near the abattoirs of Vaugirard, a no-man's-land between town and country, a sort of hide-out for aspiring artists for whom fame still lay in wait. He met others marked out by fate — Blaise Cendrars, Canudo, Apollinaire, Max Jacob, André Salmon — names which magically avoke the atmosphere of the period.

In May 1914 Chagall left Paris, stopped in Berlin for the opening of an exhibition of his works at the Galerie Sturm and on 15th June arrived in Russia to attend his sister's wedding and to find Bella, whom he shortly after married.

★ ★ ★

In 1923 he returned to France, after living through the Revolution (as we have already described) and after several months in Berlin, trying in vain to recover the pictures he had left there in 1914. In France he rediscovered the free expansion and fulfilment which were so essential to him. With all his early works lost, he reconstructed his past, strengthening his links with it by repainting his old pictures from memory and from sketches. Once again he plunged into the current stream of painting, but as always without subscribing to any one school, not even to the newly-born surrealism which he had himself heralded, and with which he was associated, though for him it was too automatic to be satisfying. He discovered the French countryside, stayed first at Ile Adam, then at Montchauvet, and strengthened his ties with France, which were not simply those of artistic choice but of a deeper, emotional affinity. In 1926 he rediscovered the Côte d'Azur, and when eleven years later he became a French citizen this was only the consecration of a union long-since consummated.

In 1940 he moved to Gordes, and then to Marseilles, in the hope of evading the German Occupation, but without success. He was arrested, and only released after considerable difficulties. Finally he accepted from the Americans both protection and an invitation to the U.S.A. In May, 1941, after lengthy hesitation, he left Marseilles for Lisbon and thence for New York, where he arrived in late June.

★ ★ ★

Chagall's third French period started in 1947. This time he was no longer a stranger seeking a propitious haven, but in a way a prodigal son joyfully received by his family on his return, garlanded with adventures and memories, and crowned with a glory which surmounted frontiers and mundane affairs. In fact, the battle was over; Chagall's destiny was accomplished and there remained only for him to maintain the promise inherent in this sequence of experiences and to reap their harvest. The returning Chagall assumed in Paris his definitive personality as a modest yet triumphant man, who in success does not forget his origins and seems slightly puzzled by the fame for which he has in fact always hoped. A grand exhibition of his work was held in the Musée National d'Art Moderne in Paris, and a room was reserved for him in the French pavilion at the Venice Biennale. He lived for several months at Orgeval, near Saint Germain en Laye, in a house as exciting and fantastic as his pictures, a house which seemed to be on the point of dissolving into the surrounding verdure. Soon, in 1949, he moved back to the South of France, and in 1950 settled at Vence in the sunshine of the Côte d'Azur. From then on, the Maeght Gallery has organized regular exhibitions of his work.

ARABIAN NIGHTS, 1946 (Kamar al Zaman and the Dervish)   45
Gouache 23 ½" × 16"   Private collection, Sweden

The Circus   Lithograph   1960

Blue Still Life   Lithograph 7^1/$_2$″ × 9^1/$_2$″ *From the exhibition "Derrière le Miroir" ("Behind the Mirror")*
Published by Aimé Maeght, 1957

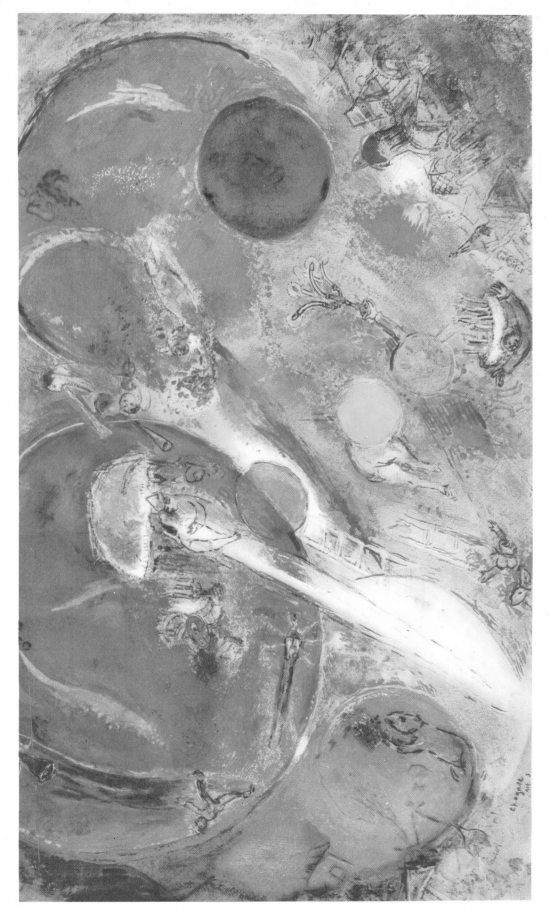

"The Firebird", Set for Act III of Stravinsky's Ballet: The Wedding-Feast, 1945 Gouache 14 3/4" × 24 3/8" Artist's collection

"The Firebird", Sketch for the Curtain for Stravinsky's Ballet, 1945   Gouache 14 $\frac{3}{4}$" × 24 $\frac{3}{8}$"   Artist's collection

In the Cafe, 1930 Oil 14″ × 6″ Artist's collection

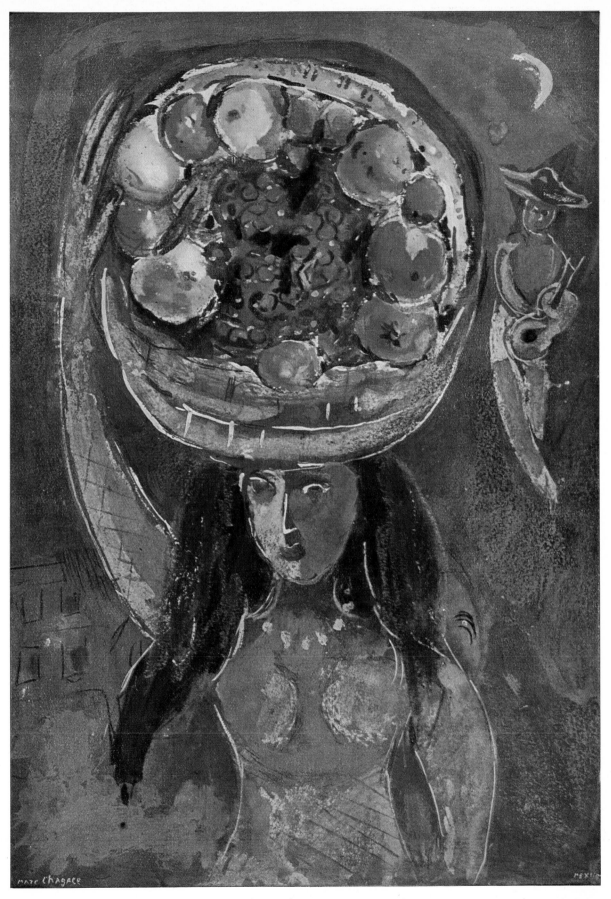

THE FRUIT-BASKET. MEXICO, 1942   Gouache 23 ½″ × 16″   Cone collection, Baltimore Museum of Art

THE RUE DE LA PAIX, 1953
52   Oil on canvas 37¼″ × 31½″   Private collection, Paris

BLUE VIOLINIST, 1947 Oil 32¼″ ×25″ Collection of Mrs. James McLane, Los Angeles, California

WOMAN WITH GREEN DONKEY, circa 1961
Oil 13″ × 28 ½″   Collection of Mr. and Mrs. W. Staehelin, Zurich

THE CANTICLE I, 1957
Oil $55\,^{1}/_{8}{''} \times 64\,^{1}/_{2}{''}$ Artist's collection

In 1952 he met Valentine Brodsky, whom he married on 12th July, and from then on his whole life and artistic creation took on a definitive character. His deliberate happiness reached the peak of self-expansion, and at his most skilful he preserves the charm and mystery of a lover's wonder. His emotional life — always a strong influence on his art — now harmonized with it more than ever before to create a mature serenity and sense of security without his becoming either self-satisfied or smugly middle-class. His art has not atrophied, yet no deep change has taken place. Rather he has reached a moment of calm affirmation, of free play with forms and colours, of which after all his previous experiments he is now a master, a moment when richness of style and material becomes overwhelmingly simple, when science seems natural and everything is possible because it is easy — enormous canvases, ceramics, stained-glass, engravings — when there is no need to try to establish the distinctions between the spiritual and the material.

★ ★ ★

AMERICA. — America received him in 1941, and awarded him the Carnegie Prize in 1939. Chagall may have escaped from his nationalities (Russian and French) when he went to the New World, but he never forgot them. He arrived without memories and without plans, almost against his will, yet armed with all that his earlier years had given him. There he met the American vision of himself and found he was of international stature, an official member of the rescued élite, yet he felt ill-suited to this role. The emotions and dimensions of the New World were foreign to him, and also its great confusion of past and future, new ideas and old traditions.

For some time Chagall remained bewildered and misunderstood, ill-prepared for his new way of life and disturbed by events in Europe. He had left France occupied by the Germans, and the day he arrived in New York Hitler invaded Russia, making him feel doubly vulnerable. Yet here he became a public figure, a star whose performances, even when severely criticized or uncomprehended, were more important than those of someone unknown. As his own monument and symbol he felt very ill at ease, in spite of the kindnesses and attentions pressed on him. The process of acclimatization was eased by the presence of his wife Bella and his daughter Ida, by having brought some of his pictures with him and by finding in New York some other European refugees, including Lionello Venturi, the Maritains and Pierre Matisse, Henri Matisse's son, who had settled there as a picture-dealer.

In spite of these attachments, Chagall at first felt lost, and only began to find himself again when he visited Mexico after the choreographer Massine had asked him to design the sets and costumes for his ballet *Aleko*. In the primitive ways and colourful art of the Mexicans he found something very closely related to his own nature, and having made sketches for this ballet in New York, he executed all the colour detail for the sets in Mexico.

The following year, 1943, saw yet another link forged with his past: a Russian Cultural Mission arrived in the U.S., giving Chagall a chance to renew his old friendship with the actor Michoels and the poet Itzik Feffer. At this time he was working on paintings he had brought from France, altering them and giving them a new definition. Current events had a great influence on him, and to this period belong his canvases on the subject of the Crucifixion and his scenes of war, betraying the concern he felt in spite of his own material security. In 1944 came a personal tragedy, too, into his life, when Bella, who had been in bad health for some while, died suddenly on 2nd September of a virus infection. For months Chagall did no work, but helped his daughter Ida to translate into French,

Motherhood   *Wash-drawing 30" × 22¹/₂"*

Bella's memoirs, which appeared under the title *Lumières Allumées — Shining Lights*. When he resumed painting his first pictures were concerned with preserving Bella's memory.

During the summer of 1945 he was given another opportunity to work in the theatre, and rediscovered his old enthusiasm and vigorous colours in the designs for Stravinsky's *Firebird*. Once more also he took up the alteration and completion of old pictures, bringing to them a self-assurance and affirmation, often combined with a great simplicity derived from the sum of his previous experiences, as much in his choice of themes as in his composition or his colours. In 1946 the Museum of Modern Art in New York held a large exhibition embracing 40 years of his work, from which one gathered a complete impression of the nature of his artistic output. It was as though, shortly before his departure for France, America gave Chagall the opportunity to draw up his balance-sheet.

In the same year he returned to Paris, but only for a few months. He immediately renewed old friendships and made new ones, and in spite of all the changes which had taken place he revived his private life there which had been temporarily interrupted. He found he was even more deeply attached than before, not only to the atmosphere of Paris, but to the city itself, to its houses and its views. He returned only temporarily to America and came back to Paris in the autumn of 1947 to attend the opening of the exhibition of his works at the Musée National d'Art Moderne which we have already mentioned.

★ ★ ★

America, France and Russia, but particularly the last two, form the background for the various stages of Chagall's life which we have just summarized. But Chagall has also travelled widely, and often brought back some new influence from the various places he visited. In 1933 he travelled to Holland, England, Italy and Spain. Above all in Israel, where he has stayed many times since 1931, he has found a country and its customs, quite apart from his warm reception there, which touched a chord in his innermost being. In Greece, which he visited in 1952 and 1954, he discovered a sense of balance and lightness which undoubtedly helped to give his style its present assured and definitive air.

HIS TECHNIQUES

COLOUR. — In all his work and at all stages of his life it is Chagall's colours which attract and capture one's attention. In his early years his range was limited by his emphasis on form, to which the colour gives fullness, density and texture, and thanks to its physical presence his early pictures never give the impression of painted drawings, in spite of the clarity and force of the outlines. The colours are a living, integral part of the picture and are never passively flat, or banal like an afterthought. They sculpt and animate the volume of the shapes in the pictures, though they soon show some degree of independence from them. They indulge in flights of fancy and invention which do not exactly follow the design but add new perspectives and graduated, blended tones. His colours do not even attempt to imitate nature but rather to suggest movements, planes and rhythms.

This tendency was accentuated when Chagall arrived in France, particularly when he came in contact with cubism, where colours are divided into precisely defined areas without necessarily following the contours of figures or objects. This rigid formula becomes much more supple and more imaginative in Chagall's hands, and he applied it more methodically when he returned to Russia, where the problems of executing murals and stage designs most probably intervened in this wish to create a freely rhythmic space, more instinctive than actual.

This superficially geometric method was for Chagall only a passing phase. Almost immediately after his return to France he resumed an infinitely freer, more flexible style and colours just as bold yet more subtle. Sometimes he even adopted a system of large planes, or rather huge patches of the same colour, to whose surface he managed to give a semblance of fluidity. Clearly from this moment on the manipulation and blending of colours has been his prime concern, so that he probably even paints them onto the canvas before shaping them into a precise form.

In his most recent period form and design in a picture are hardly necessary, but serve simply as a clue to its message. Even so design and colouring may not coincide, but are often superimposed without following the same lines. All Chagall's art is contained in the colour, which is his miraculous way of suggesting and affirming simultaneously; giving the spectator the feeling of participation in an apparently unfettered dream, though in fact the artist does impose his own vision with unquestionable authority.

Chagall's first colours — warm and gleaming with the mellow glow of a charcoal fire, softened by the ash — have gradually extended their range to become the now familiar fireworks which can convey a whirl of brilliance with the use of two or three tones. Chagall is unrivalled in this ability to give a vivid impression of explosive movement with the simplest use of colours.

Throughout his artistic life, but most of all in recent years, Chagall's colours have created a vibrant atmosphere which is in fact his own personal vision, remote from comparison with any lines of perspective. He can arrange all the sections of his picture on the same plane with uniform density. It is very probable that this technique assisted in the execution of murals like the ceiling at the Paris Opéra, or of stage designs, since in this field he succeeded in creating an indefinite area, neither blocked by a flat surface nor yet limitless in scope, thus preserving a certain realism which still does not preclude fantasy.

In his earlier paintings Chagall's colours were thick and opaque in texture, but gradually lightened to an ethereal brilliance. His later oils, gouaches and coloured lithographs all belong to the same style. His use of different materials throws his technique into relief, and the results are all very similar, being expressed in an idiom which the artist found wholly satisfying, because it left him complete freedom to exercise his virtuosity — a virtuosity which might appear facile, even involuntary, but which was in fact the apogee of all his knowledge.

Through his very personal mediums of expression Chagall has arrived to-day, with his idea of the evocation of space, at a very similar point to that attained by Matisse. If their styles differ, their mastery is the same, and in both cases was achieved only through an amazing knowledge of colour and the inter-relationship of shades and tones, to which the needs of photographic perspective and design take second place.

* * *

DRAWING AND ENGRAVING. — It is both difficult and artificial to distinguish Chagall the draftsman from Chagall the engraver, not because he ignores the special techniques of engraving and simply draws on copper or stone, but because on the contrary he well understands the potentialities and requirements of each craft and deploys them skilfully to reach a personal mode of expression. However his method in these two different genres certainly springs from the same conception of a sketch, and of the possibilities inherent in the use of black and white in contrast — or in harmony — with painting, in which as we have already seen colour is his main concern. One can discern the painter in Chagall just by studying his use of black and white.

CHRIST, 1950 Gouache 11 1/8″ × 9″ Private collection, France

The Flute-player, 1957   Lithograph 10" × 16½"   Published by Maeght, Paris

In his years of apprenticeship, drawing was indissolubly bound to painting, and he outlined both shapes and colours. When he arrived in France and came under the influence of cubism the drawing became more important, as he sketched in new structures and divided and harmonized the composition of a picture into geometric shapes, which were then softened by his brush. He stressed the composition of a picture without minimizing the function of the colour, and his work at this time seems more like an inventive exercise or a display of sensitive intuition than adherence to theories. Unlike the cubists, Chagall never found it necessary to dissect reality in order to reconstruct it; on the contrary he remained faithful to fact, and used for instance an emotional episode for a plastic purpose, without having the slightest intention of serving reality.

When Chagall returned to Russia in 1914 and became involved in the problems of mural decoration and theatrical design, draftsmanship again occupied a prominent place in his rediscovered, re-imagined folklore, as he adapted popular traditions to a new style. In this period his drawing was hard, precise, linear — the opposite of his earlier work in Russia, when his shapes were swathed in a soft embrace, and his colours bounded by a thick soft outline.

Chagall made his first engravings during the months he spent in Berlin before returning to France in 1922. A publisher, Paul Cassirer, proposed using them as copper-plate illustrations to the memoirs Chagall had just completed, but the translation proved so difficult that finally an album appeared containing only the engravings.

After these first experiments, Chagall became so interested in the new processes that he tried them all, abandoning painting for several months, except for a few water-colours. He started on dry-point and nitric acid etching, lithographs and even wood-cuts. About thirty copper-plates, as many lithographs and five wood-cuts resulted from this period, and not only showed the affinity which Chagall now felt connected and differentiated painting and engraving, but also demonstrated his need to maintain contact with his past. We have already mentioned his reconstruction of his lost paintings and thus of his own traditional universe. A similar feeling guided him, justified by his subject (the story of his life), and helped him to rediscover episodes from his youth and to crystallize once more these mental images. In his first plates one already sees the importance of man in these compositions — man seen in familiar acts of everyday life — and how Chagall both follows reality and interprets it freely.

Detached from the magic of colours, his strokes seem sharper and more incisive, and his observation of humanity is almost cruel in its candour, without ever being malicious or morbid. In his very exaggerations one senses compassion for his characters and understanding of their absurdities and excesses. He is moved by their ineptness as though he felt involved in their human drama — at once actor and spectator. This is no doubt why his most improbable poses, situations and compositions have an irrefutable truth.

His engravings hardly contain any trace of geometric dissection in the cubist style, which was to be found a few months earlier in his theatrical designs. Here the storyteller resumed his rightful place and the man his dreams, arranging his subjects according to his wholly individual order, which, however fantastic, soon becomes familiar. Chagall almost always introduces a little humour into the emotions of his paintings, probably to avoid an appearance of sentimentality. His lithographs from this period more resemble the drawings from his earlier years in Russia, in their density, the flexibility of the surrounding strokes, their sinuous lines and coarse, granulated texture, which is caused by the lithographic stilo or ink and are more closely related to painting than copper-plate can ever be.

LOVERS AND FLOWERS   Gouache 25 ½″ × 19 ¾″   Collection of Berthold Ullmann, Basle

When Chagall returned to France in 1923, his friend Blaise Cendrars introduced him to Vollard, a publisher who was planning some deluxe editions and who asked him to illustrate a volume. Chagall suggested Gogol's *Dead Souls*, to which Vollard agreed. Chagall probably chose this for the same reason that his engravings for his memoirs are so moving: because it gave him a chance to revive his memories of Russia, in lively interiors with furniture and possessions and picturesque characters, and in village streets with wooden houses. He still remembered so much at first-hand to supply his imagination that between 1923 and 1927 he executed seven hundred plates. This time he abandoned the soft strokes of dry-point etching and only used nitric acid, with its neat tracery of supple, calligraphic arabesques and the opportunity it offered him to create shades and textures which resemble painting.

The subjects of *Ma vie* and *Dead Souls* are bound to Chagall's personality inasmuch as it is in turn bound to Russia. When Vollard next asked Chagall to illustrate the *Fables* of La Fontaine, he was probably thinking of the artist's affinity with French life and legends. Without being disloyal to his motherland, Chagall was beginning to feel more and more at ease in his adopted country, as he tasted more deeply than on his first visit its essential tender warmth, which appealed so well to the emotional side of his nature.

The first intention was to make coloured gouaches which could be translated into copper-plate engravings, but it soon became apparent that Chagall's very style and his freedom, as much as his skill with transparencies, would make such a transposition difficult. Leaving the gouaches to stand as independent works, Chagall decided to start again with his illustrations as black and white copper-plates. He brought to this an infinitely more flexible technical skill than he had achieved before. He began this enormous task between 1927 and 1930, and spread it over several years. Between 1931 and its completion in 1939 he executed five hundred etchings, of which 39 were re-engraved between 1952 and 1956.

In *Dead Souls* the artist was already exploring compromise solutions involving the simultaneous use of glaze and dry-point. In the *Fables* his blending of techniques is even more skilled and the effects are both more subtle and more positive. His whites are more glowing, his blacks deeper, and neither is ever an inert patch of light or shade, but quivers with life. The composition is more elaborate and the plates contain more detail. In earlier works one often thought in terms of a design executed from notes or even from marginal jottings, but in the *Fables* whole pages have been created expressly for the book, to provide a visually realistic texture. As always a story is no limitation to Chagall, but could even be called a stimulant; however he is less dominated by it here than previously, and now conveys more the general spirit and feeling than the details.

In some Biblical illustrations which he began after a journey to Egypt and Palestine in 1931, Chagall again widened his ideas and media. His illustrations for books of Russian stories are made of memories; those for La Fontaine are truly French; but those for the Bible are more detached from time and place, although Chagall did not want to undertake them until he had seen the countryside of the Holy Land. He accumulated there no sheaf of sketches, but something much deeper — a way of feeling and of sublimating shapes and beings. These three series of works strangely symbolize the three essential stages in Chagall's inner development: the growth of his vision which passed gradually from familiar events to loftier symbolism without apparent break or contradiction. A study of the artist's engravings possibly gives a clearer explanation of his continuity and development than do his paintings. Though his black and white plates often look as though he had coloured them strongly, the colour is only truly effective in those lithographs which he retouched after a lapse of several years. Thirteen lithographs which he executed for a New York publisher to illustrate an edition of the *Thousand and One Nights* strongly resemble the sets and costumes he had just designed for the Ballets *Aleko* and *The Firebird*, not only in their colouring but in their inspiration and the pleasing element of fantasy — an element into which Chagall perhaps fled to escape his troubled memories and to protest against the disturbances and materialism of the world.

From then on virtually all his engravings were lithographs. As in his work on copper, he discovered technical possibilities different from those inherent in painting, yet very similar in their realisation. and his style became extremely complex: a blend of strong, fleshy textures, thick outlines (to stress form and movement), light hatching and great precision in some of the details without any loss of stylistic unity.

Since this period Chagall's art has been far removed from so-called " popular imagery ", and a study of these works will show how inaccurate — or at least inadequate — is the frequent application of this term to him. His mind and his sources of inspiration are of course " popular ": that is, they have the initial freshness associated with simple people, but they are used to serve a laboriously acquired artistry by techniques which are suited to it rather than by means of formal teaching. Through Chagall's engravings one comes to understand more clearly the machinery of this slow process of study, the result of which is that he has remained true to his birthright, experiencing the most challenging artistic movements of this century and even being associated with them, without ever betraying his own individuality.

DESIGNING

MAJOR DECORATIVE DESIGNS. — It has been said much too often that Chagall's art is that of a visual story-teller adept at sumptuous illustrations for authors who are unable to fire one's imagination unaided. To think this is not to belittle his imagination or scope, but the size of his works. He has categorically refuted this imputation by executing several enormous compositions which are not just enlarged pictures, but can be studied in conjunction with the surrounding spaces and architecture.

He found many opportunities to demonstrate his exceptional talent for the theatre. Indeed the instinctive, magical quality to be found throughout his works was here completely at home, and nowhere can the marriage of the real and the fantastic be so aptly applied than in the theatre, where artificiality becomes truth and fancy logic. His first stage designs were executed in Russia during the period after 1914, at the time of that amazing revision of scenic aesthetics under Meyerhold and Taïroff, when static ideas of stage design were being swept away in favour of a wholly arbitrary sense of space with different dimensions, perspectives, colours and rhythms.

Nothing could have appealed more strongly to Chagall at that time, drawn as he was by the geometric discoveries of cubism and his own urge to enliven them with a freer and more detached imagination. His dreams sprang to life and became an actual movement. The Jewish playwrights such as Gogol, Evreïnoff and Singe offered him popular and imaginative themes which well matched his temperament. Working at the Kamerny Theatre with the stage director Granowsky he found his freest expression, and progressed to an even deeper involvement in theatrical creation by trying to make the actors understand the psychological and plastic implications of his sets, so that the rhythms of their acting would harmonize with the rhythms of his designs.

Chagall played a significant role in Russian artistic life at this time, both through his murals — commissioned for Vitebsk and Moscow — and through his stage designs, and was one of the most important

66

The Sun at Vence, 1962   Wash   Maeght Gallery, Paris

The Pink Painter, 1959   Lithograph 19 ³/₄″ × 26 ¹/₈″
Poster design for the Exhibition at the Musée des Arts Décoratifs, Paris

LA BAIE DES ANGES, 1962 Gouache 22$\frac{1}{6}$″ × 26$\frac{1}{6}$″ Poster design for the town of Nice

Notre Dame and the Eiffel Tower 11 ¹/₄″ × 14 ³/₄″

The Musical Clown, 1957   Lithograph 26¹/₂″ × 18¹/₂″
Poster design for the Exhibition at the Maeght Gallery, Paris

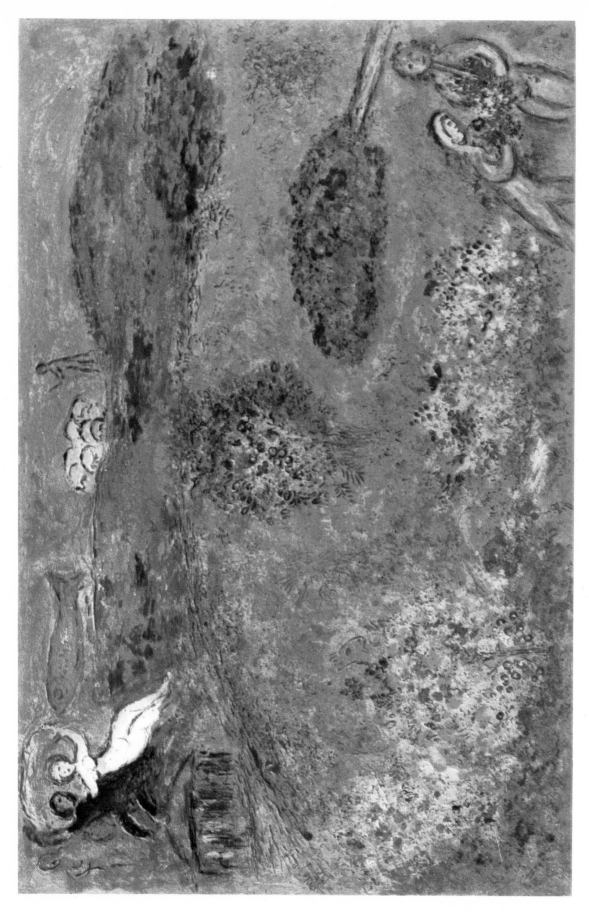

"The Orchard" Lithograph for Longus's work "Daphnis et Chloë". Published by Tériade, Paris, 1961

forces in the current urge towards anti-realism, helping towards the new Russia's astonishingly inventive creations. While designing sets for the Jewish plays he also painted murals for the foyer of the new Jewish Theatre in Moscow. These huge canvases can already be discussed as a fluid ensemble which conveys a considerable maturity. They take the place of the figures, gestures and symbols with which he had previously experimented and which appear again in his later works: animals, musicians dancers — the familiar vehicles for his ideas. Chagall's rejection of all arbitrary form is both striking and natural, and whereas it still surprises one in a small painting it seems completely right and logical in a theatrical design, where it creates an illusory atmosphere which is the very essence of a theatrical performance, and establishes its freedom from the limitations of realism. Here theatrical dynamism reaches its climax of anti-realistic truth.

For some while after leaving Russia, Chagall had no opportunity for tackling the problems of stage design, but the harlequins, clowns and acrobats who constantly appear in his paintings at this time convey his sentimental attachment to and nostalgia for the theatre. His first return to this sphere was in 1942, in America, when Massine asked him to design the sets and costumes for the ballet *Aleko*, based on a story of Pushkin's, with music by Tchaikovsky. This gave him a welcome opportunity to leave the unfamiliar atmosphere of the U.S. and to visit Mexico. In 1945 he was commissioned to design the sets and costumes for Stravinsky's *The Firebird*.

These successes contributed greatly towards establishing Chagall's reputation in America. They differ completely from the ideas being introduced into the Russian theatre some twenty years previously. The abrupt rhythms of cubism are gone, and Chagall immerses the spectator in a luminous, coloured fairy-land where forms are mistily defined and the spaces themselves seem animated with whirlwinds or explosions. This triumph of theatrical colour technique reached its climax in his designs for the Paris production of Ravel's *Daphnis et Chloë* in 1958.

Chagall's gift for animating an imaginary space, which so exactly fits the requirements of the theatre, is again apparent in his repainting of the ceiling of the Paris Opéra, which he did at the request of the Minister of Culture, André Malraux. This was a most adventurous enterprise and before it was even begun had raised a lively controversy. When it was finished in 1964 many of its original opponents abandoned their prejudices, saying they had never thought it could harmonize with a building of such a positive and different period. In fact it modifies the general impact of the hall without spoiling its rhythms, and the brilliant new colours seem to brighten the surrounding gilt-work. Besides, the previous, very academic ceiling had so to speak completed the confines of the theatre, while Chagall's work on the contrary rejects the idea of sealing the shrine, and creates a vague outline with a quantity of imprecise figures and no false perspectives, so that its limits seem to stretch into infinity.

★ ★ ★

CERAMICS AND SCULPTURE. — One should never forget, even in Chagall's most academic and sophisticated works, that his temperament is basically that of a peasant, even a craftsman, which fact explains his fascination with new techniques and hence to a large extent his interest in engraving, in theatrical design, in the details of costume-making, and in experimenting with stained-glass, in which field he works closely on his sketches with the glazier, painting drafts and altering the density of the glass in order to mould the colours correctly.

The fashion for ceramics on the Côte d'Azur since the last war understandably attracted Chagall's attention. Workshops sprang up at Antibes, Vence and Vallauris, and Chagall naturally accepted the

THE PAINTER AND THE PALETTE, 1952 Lithograph 23″ × 19″ Published by Aimé Maeght, Paris

74

THE THREE ACROBATS, 1956 Original lithograph 24 3/4″ × 18 3/4″

challenge, as did Picasso and Fernand Léger. At first he painted existing pieces of pottery, but soon felt the need to go a stage further and design his own. This was the beginning of his work as a sculptor, a complementary activity to his painting.

From the start he treated the same subjects as in his pictures, for instance pairs of lovers or animals, adapting them for the new medium though they seem as freely deployed as ever. He immediately comprehended the exigencies of this technique, but found in them an exciting challenge. He uses the convex and concave surfaces like colours and textures and, due no doubt to his experience as an engraver, he uses a quantity of fine lines for some of his shading effects, either to penetrate the glaze and show the raw material through it, or to intensify the colour.

After experimenting with pots and dishes (exhibited by Maeght in 1950) Chagall moved from designing and decorating accessories to mural ceramics, without however finding any great satisfaction in the square segments used for large surfaces. The geometrical divisions disturbed him by their regularity, because it imposed on him a discipline which prevented the creation of a plastic image. He did however willingly accept the use of lead in stained-glass, and learned to exploit it most effectively, though regular, rectangular divisions failed to stimulate his imagination. This led to his abandoning mural ceramics in 1952, after an exhibition at Maeght's Gallery of some beautiful pieces which he had created with Madoura at Vallauris.

He returned to sculpted shapes of his own invention, but these he started to mould according to the theme painted on each one, rather than treating them as shapes with decoration. The objects soon lost their practical usefulness, so that in his hands ceramics became sculpture — like painting, a medium for plastic expression, independent of material, utilitarian necessity — or rather a transition from the planes of painting to the volumes of sculpture. So successful was this transition that he was soon working in stone itself, where again his unsophisticated approach and consideration for the requirements of his material guided him and helped him to find a compromise between the liberty of an art and the restrictions of a craft. His sculptures are like the capitals of medieval columns: however complex their construction they are confined to predetermined spatial limits, and adhere to these rules. Above all in the problems of ceramics and sculpture does Chagall's material and spiritual progress resemble that of Gauguin. This is hardly a question of influence, however remote, in spite of Chagall's admiration for Gauguin, but simply a clear parallel in the evolution of their senses and minds. As each artist approached a new stage, striving to surpass his previous achievements, he found himself faced with fresh problems and was drawn into new spheres of art. They both seemed all the more original and effective because they entered spontaneously on each new technique, conscious of its exigencies yet without the burden of tradition, simply seeking to realize the same effects as they had sought in painting. This analogy is also justified by their similar reaction to rigid, arbitrary systems in vogue among their contemporaries, namely to rehabilitate subject-matter, not for its own sake, but for its sensuous content, without excluding a rational consideration of technical as well as spiritual values.

★ ★ ★

STAINED GLASS. — Chagall has made some significant contributions to monumental art in his work on stained glass. In retrospect it seems self-evident that his style would lead to success in this fields because of his taste for intense yet fresh colours, their interplay with light and refraction in rhythms of their own. In the same way his theatrical work proved that his colours could stand the brightest glare of light, which seemed to bring out their true values and never make them seem pale and faded.

76

THE BLUE CIRCUS, 1950-52   Oil 92″ × 71″   Artist's collection

FOR VAVA, 1955   Gouache 25 ¹/₄″ × 19″   Collection of Vava Chagall, Vence

PORTRAIT OF VAVA, 1955-56   Oil 37$\frac{1}{2}$″ × 28$\frac{1}{2}$″   Collection of Vava Chagall, Vence

LIFE, 1964 Oil $116\,^1\!/_2{}'' \times 159\,^1\!/_2{}''$
Maeght Foundation, Saint-Paul-de-Vence

▷

STUDY OF A VIOLINIST, 1952
Brush and Chinese ink

THE TRIBE OF DAN, 1960 Final Sketch for one of the windows of the Hadassah Synagogue,
near Jerusalem 16$\frac{1}{2}$″ × 12$\frac{1}{2}$″ Private collection

THE TRIBE OF ZEBULUN, 1960 Final Sketch for one of the windows of the Hadassah Synagogue,
near Jerusalem Gouache 16$\frac{1}{2}$″ × 12$\frac{1}{2}$″ Private collection

Moses, 1960   Lithograph 19 ³/₄″ × 26 ¹/₂″ for the exhibition "Windows for Metz Cathedral, 1960"

THE TRIBE OF LEVI, 1961   Window for the Hadassah Synagogue, near Jerusalem   133″ × 98 ½″

TURQUOISE PLATE, 1956   Ceramic

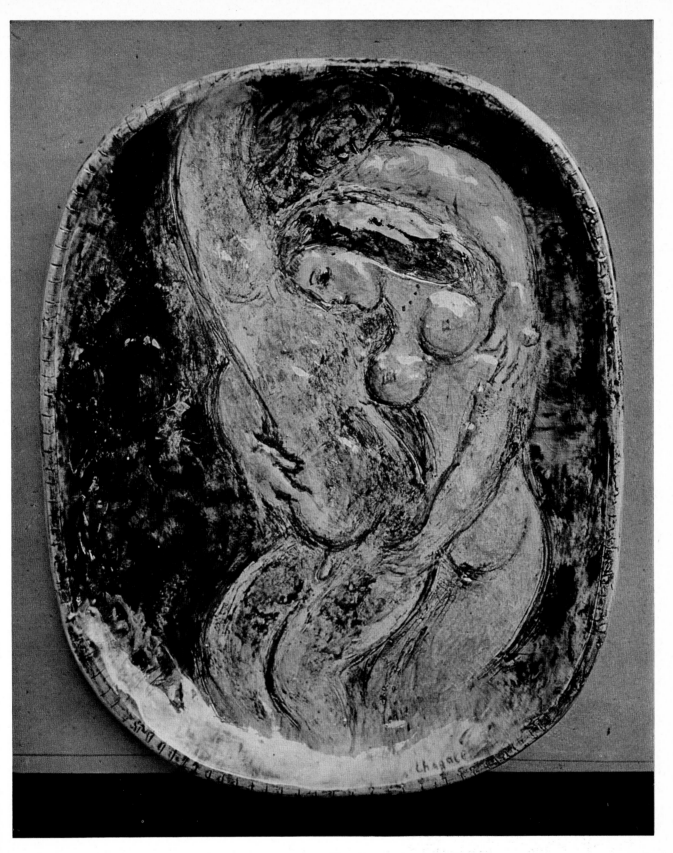

THE LOVERS, 1956 Ceramic

WINDOW FOR METZ CATHEDRAL (fragment), 1959-60

In spite of all these indications, he was not invited to design any stained glass until quite late in life. In 1956 he was commissioned to make two windows for the church at Assy, which he approached with diffidence, using colour discreetly and preferring grisailles on plain glass. From 1958 to 1960 when working for Metz Cathedral however, he became bolder, accepted the limitations imposed by the architecture and the vicinity of other, ancient windows, and tried to find harmonies as clear as those of the old masters. He never tried to imitate his own painting, but found a colour formula which was exactly suitable for the new technique, and fitted naturally into each work while still belonging within his own tradition.

His greatest work in this field is a cycle of twelve large windows for the Hadassah Hospital Synagogue, near Jerusalem. The subject was the twelve tribes of Israel, which Chagall illustrated with symbols and animals, not with human figures. This is one of the most important modern works of art — a luminous fantasy, executed with great precision, with the light values he uses in his paintings modified so that they are accurately reproduced in this medium where such values are determined by the glass itself and its different degrees of transparency.

In his murals and stage designs Chagall made surfaces seem alive, but in his stained glass the wall itself vanishes and the whole interior is filled with radiance, as though the spectator is himself a part of this source of intense, multi-coloured light.

HIS SUBJECT-MATTER

If one can trace the smooth parabola of an artist's spiritual life by studying the stages of his physical existence and the various aspects of his creative work, as we have previously done, one can surely also do so by noting the different subjects he has used and by seeking the connections between them and his motives for choosing them. We have seen that above and beyond the often arbitrary changes of circumstance in Chagall's life, certain elements in his art remain permanent, recurring with calm persistence at every stage and linking the various phases to each other.

The same theory can be applied to his choice of subject and method of treatment. The most obviously constant element is his gift for happiness and his instinctive compassion, which even in the most serious subjects prevents him from dramatization, and helps him to pass through difficult moments without apparent discouragement. Musicians have figured at every stage of his work. Since Bella's first incursion into his life lovers have sought each other, embraced, caressed, floated through the air, met in wreaths of flowers, stretched, and swooped like the melodious passage of their vivid day-dreams. Acrobats contort themselves with the grace of exotic flowers on the end of their stems; flowers and foliage abound everywhere.

Another characteristic of Chagall is his gift of narration, discernible from his earliest paintings. He progressed from the particular to the general: his pictures of Vitebsk are realistic and give the impression of firsthand experience; they capture a fleeting moment of action, almost a dramatic incident. Chagall's facility in narration, one's pleasure in listening to him and his pleasure in enumerating detail are definitely characteristic of a genuine raconteur, who knows how to utilize a picturesque detail in the composition of a coherent, plastic whole. He has never neglected these gifts, even when his tales are less meticulously detailed; even when they are on a loftier plane (for instance his Biblical stories) or when his gentle or cruel animals, his musicians, women and flowers parade across imagined spaces above the roof-tops.

With a logic all his own, Chagall blends the real and the fantastic in a metamorphosis which is disconcerting, yet attractive enough to be acceptable. The freedom with which he depicts his men and beasts he brings also to his landscapes: his earlier ones were inspired by the streets of Vitebsk and certain Russian villages, and his recent ones by Paris and Provence. Nowhere does he attempt a realistic presentation, but in spite of the element of fantasy one recognizes the original, more by the evocation of atmosphere than by physical accuracy.

Chagall's most persistent subject is life itself, in its simplicity or its hidden complexity. He has no liking for pedantic allegories, nor for still lifes. He presents for our study places, people and objects from his own life — Russian log-huts or the Eiffel Tower, great moments in human life (birth, marriage, love and death), symbols which give extra significance to animate and inanimate objects and which gradually become more familiar and more serene. The steady growth of this feeling of serenity can be traced through his work to the dominant position which it has now held for many years. Chagall has outlived the dramas of his life and reached a point of balance — a moment when he has assimilated his troubles and all his creation has reached fulfilment.

Ceiling of the Paris Opéra, 1964 (Fragment)   Photo Mourlot Frères, Paris

BIOGRAPHIE

BIOGRAPHY

1887. Birth of Marc Chagall, on 7th July, at Vitebsk, Russia.

1906. Studied under the painter Penn.

1907. Entered the Imperial College for Furtherance of the Arts, St. Petersburg.

1908. Léon Bakst, in whose studio he worked, introduced him to French painting.

1909. Vinaver, a member of the Douma, offered him a scholarship to study in Rome or Paris with 125 francs per month. First meeting with Bella.

1910. Left for Paris. First settled in the Impasse du Maine.

1911-12. Moved to the artists' town called "La Ruche", where became friendly with Cendrars, Canudo and Apollinaire. Exhibited in the Salon des Indépendants and the Salon d'Automne.

1914. Thanks to Apollinaire, solo exhibition of his works arranged at Gallery Sturm, Berlin. Chagall attended this on his way to St. Petersburg to rejoin his fiancée, Bella. The war kept him in Russia, where he was called up into a camouflage unit, and remained in St. Petersburg.

1915. Married Bella. Exhibited in Moscow.

1917. Russian Revolution. Chagall appointed Commissar for Fine Arts for Vitebsk; founded Academy there, with Lissitzky, Pougny and later Malevitch as teachers.

1918. Organized celebrations for the anniversary of the October Revolution. An entire room in the Winter Palace in Leningrad reserved for Chagall's works, which were all bought by the State.

1919-20. Mural paintings and stage designs for the "New State Jewish Theatre". Discussions and increasing disagreement with Malevitch at the Vitebsk Academy. Chagall offered his resignation for the first time, withdrew it, but in 1920 resigned directorship of the Academy and moved to Moscow, where he enlarged his theatrical activities.

1921. Became teacher in a colony of war-orphans near Moscow.

1922. Left Russia and returned to France via Berlin, where he failed to recover his pictures. Cassirer commissioned engravings from him to illustrate his autobiography, entitled *Ma Vie* (*My Life*).

1923. Settled in Paris. Introduced to Vollard who commissioned him to illustrate Gogol's *Dead Souls*.

1924. First retrospective exhibition in Paris, at the Barbazanges-Hodebert Gallery. Stayed in Brittany, at Ile Bréhat.

1925. Stayed at Montchauvet.

1926. Stayed at the Mourillon near Toulon, and at Lake Chambon in Auvergne. Vollard commissioned illustrations for the *Fables* of La Fontaine. First exhibition in New York. Exhibited at the Granoff Gallery in Paris.

1927. Gouaches commissioned by Vollard on the subject of the circus. Stayed in Auvergne, Savoy, the Basque country, at Limoux and at Céret.

1930. Vollard commissioned illustrations for the Bible. Exhibited at the Bernheim-Jeune Gallery.

1931. Journey to Palestine.

1932. Journey to Holland. Exhibited in Amsterdam.

1933. Exhibited at the Kunsthalle in Basle. Journey to England. Nazis burned his works at Mannheim.

1934. Journey to Spain.

1935. Journey to Poland

1937. Journey to Italy.

1938. Exhibited in Brussels.

1939. Awarded the Carnegie Prize, U.S.A.

1940. Moved to the Loire Valley, then to Gordes in the Rhône Valley.

1941. Left for the United States on the invitation of the Museum of Modern Art in New York. Exhibited in New York at Pierre Matisse's gallery.

1942. Went to Mexico. Sets and costumes for the ballet *Aleko*.

1944. Death of Bella.

1945. Sets and costumes for *The Firebird* in New York.

1946. Retrospective exhibition at the New York Museum of Modern Art and at the Chicago Art Institute. Coloured lithograph illustrations for the *Thousand and One Nights*.

1947. Returned to France. Retrospective exhibition at the Musée d'Art Moderne in Paris, which was then shown at the Municipal Museum in Amsterdam and at the Tate Gallery in London.

1948. Settled at Orgeval outside Paris. Awarded International Prize for Engraving at the Venice Biennale.

1949. Moved to St. Jean Cap Ferrat.

1950. Moved to Vence. Retrospective exhibition at the Zurich Museum. First ceramic work. (Exhibition in the Maeght Gallery.)

1951. Journey to Israel. Exhibited at the Zurich Kunsthaus and the Berne Kunsthalle; also in Jerusalem, Tel Aviv and Haifa.

1952. Married Vava Brodsky. Journey to Greece. Tériade commissioned illustrations for *Daphnis et Chloë*. Exhibited at Nice.

1953. Exhibited at Turin. Series of pictures of Paris. Exhibition of sculptures and ceramics at the Curt Valentin Gallery in New York. Exhibition of engravings in Vienna.

1954. Exhibition entitled " Paris Fantastique " at the Maeght Gallery. Second journey to Greece.

1955. Exhibited at the Kestner Society in Hanover.

1956. Exhibited in the Basle and Berne Kunsthalle, and at the Amsterdam Municipal Museum. Exhibited in Brussels.

1957. Journey to Israel. Publication of the Bible. Exhibition of engravings at the National Library in Paris and the Art Museum in Basle. Stained glass for the church at Assy. Exhibitions at the Maeght Gallery and at the Sao Paulo Biennale.

1958. Sets and costumes for *Daphnis et Chloë* at the Paris Opéra. Lectured in Chicago and Brussels.

1959. Degree of Doctor Honoris Causa conferred by Glasgow University.

1960. Windows for Metz Cathedral. Degree of Doctor Honoris Causa conferred by Brandeis University.

1961. Windows for Jerusalem. Exhibited at the Musée des Arts Décoratifs, Paris.

1962. Exhibited at the Maeght Gallery. Exhibition entitled *Chagall and the Bible* at the Geneva Museum.

1964. Exhibition of monotypes, 1961-1963, at the Gérald Cramer Gallery in Geneva. Exhibition at the Maeght Gallery entitled " Dessins et lavis " (" Drawings and Colour-washes "). Unveiling of the new ceiling at the Paris Opéra.

Pan. Wash 30 × 32 Maeght Gallery, Paris

BIBLIOGRAPHY

EFROSS A. and TUGENDHOLD J. *The Art of Marc Chagall*. Moscow, 1918.

EFROSS A. and TUGENDHOLD J. *Die Kinst Marc Chagall*. Potsdam, 1921.

DÀUBLER Th. *Marc Chagall*. Rome, 1922.

WITH Karl. *Marc Chagall*. Leipzig, 1923.

ARONSON B. *Marc Chagall*. Berlin, 1924.

Special Edition of *Sélection* – poems bu APOLLINAIRE, CENDRARS, SALMON; articles by P. FIERENS, W. GEORGE, M. RAYNAL, J. MARITAIN, A. DE RIDDER, P. COURTHION, G. CHARENSOL, J. DELTEIL, A. VOLLARD, K. WITH and A. EFROSS. Antwerp, 1926 (Hebrew edition, Tel-Aviv, 1926).

LICHTENSTEIN I. *Marc Chagall*. Paris, 1927.

SALMON A. *Chagall*. Paris, 1928.

GEORGE Waldemar. *Marc Chagall*. Paris ,1928.

FIERENS Paul. *Marc Chagall*. Paris-Antwerp, 1929.

Volume No. 6 of *Sélection*. Antwerp, 1929.

LUZZATO G. *Marc Chagall*. Milan, 1930.

SCHWOB René. *Chagall et l'Ame Juive*. Paris, 1931.

HAMMACHER A. H. *Marc Chagall*. Amsterdam, 1935.

GOLDBERG Lea. *Marc Chagall*. Tel-Aviv, 1943.

MARITAIN Raîssa. *Marc Chagall*. New York, 1943.

VENTURI Lionello. *Marc Chagall*. New York, 1945.

SWEENEY J. J. *Marc Chagall*. New York, 1946.

KUTZ Aaron. *Marc Chagall* (in Hebrew). New York, 1946.

DEGAND Léon and ELUARD Paul. *Chagall: Peintures, 1942-45*. Paris, 1947.

AYRTON Michael. *The Art of Marc Chagall*. London, 1948.

MARITAIN Raîssa. *Chagall ou l'Orage Enchanté*. Geneva, 1948.

APOLLONIO Umbro. *Chagall*. Milan, 1949.

AYRTON Michael. *Chagall*. London, 1950.

ESTIENNE Charles. *Chagall*. Paris, 1951.

KLOOMOK Dr. I. *Marc Chagall, his Life and Work*. New York, 1951.

LASSAIGNE Jacques. *Marc Chagall*. Geneva, 1952.

SCHMIDT Georg. *Chagall*. Paris 1952.

CHRIST Y. (Chagall's Drawings). Paris, 1953.

SCHMIDT Georg. *Chagall*. Basle, 1955.

GENAUER E. *Chagall*. New York, 1955.

SCHMALENBACH Werner. *Chagall*. Milan 1955.

VENTURI Lionello. *Marc Chagall*. Geneva, 1956.

VERDET A. *Marc Chagall*. Geneva, 1956.

ERBEN Walter. *Chagall*. Munich, 1957.

MEYER Franz. *Marc Chagall, L'Œuvre Gravé*. Paris, 1957.

LASSAIGNE Jacques. *Chagall* (Poèmes de Marc Chagall). Paris, 1957.

CAIN Julien. *Chagall lithographe*. Monte Carlo, 1960.

LEYMARIE Jean. *Vitraux pour Jérusalem*. Monte Carlo, 1962.

MOURLOT Fernand. *Chagall Lithographe (1957-1962)*. Monte Carlo, 1963.

MEYER Franz. *Marc Chagall*. Paris, 1964.

PRINCIPAL WORKS ILLUSTRATED BY CHAGALL

Collected Hebrew Stories, line drawings. Vilna, 1917.

CHAGALL Marc. *Mein Leben* (*My Life*), 18 etchings. Berlin, 1923.

GIRADOUX, MORAND, P. MAC ORLAN, A. SALMON, Max JACOB, LACRETELLE and KESSEL. *Les Sept Péchés Capitaux* (*The Seven Deadly Sins*), 15 dry-point etchings. Paris, 1926.

ARLAND Marcel. *Maternité* (*Motherhood*), 5 etchings. Paris, 1926.

COQUIOT G. *Suite Provinciale* (*Provincial Suite*), 92 line-drawings. Paris, 1927.

GOLL Claire and Ivan. *Poèmes d'amour* (*Love-poems*), 7 ink drawings. Paris, 1930.

CHAGALL Marc. *Ma Vie* (*My Life*), 32 drawings. Paris, 1931.

WALT Abraham. *Hebrew Songs and Poems*, 32 drawings. New York, 1938.

CHAGALL Bella. *Brennendicke Licht* (*Burning Lights*), 36 drawings. New York, 1945.

ELUARD P. *Le dur Désir de durer* (*The Lasting wish to Last*), 25 drawings and a frontispiece in colour. Paris, 1946.

The Arabian Nights, 13 coloured lithographs. New York, 1946.

CHAGALL Bella. *Die Ershte Bagegenisch* (*The First Meeting*), 36 drawings. New York, 1947.

GOGOL Nikolai. *Les Ames Mortes* (*Dead Souls*), 118 engravings. Paris, 1948.

CHAGALL Bella. *Lumières Allumées* (*Burning Lights*), 45 drawings. Geneva, 1948.

BOCCACCIO. *Les Contes* (*The Tales*), cover illustrated and washes. Paris, 1950.

Les Fables de La Fontaine (*Fables by La Fontaine*), 102 engravings. Paris, 1952.

SUZKEVER. *Sibir* (poems in Hebrew), 8 washes. Jerusalem, 1953.

The Bible, 105 engravings. Paris, 1956.

The Bible, 105 reprinted engravings and 16 original lithographs. Paris, 1956.

ILLUSTRATIONS